A Father's Letters

Connecting Past to Present

Murray Browne

Publisher: Muted Horn Communications, LLC Decatur, Georgia USA

Book Cover Art: You Can't Lay Down Your Memory Chest of Drawers, 1991, fabricated 2008. Tejo Remy (Dutch Born 1960). High Museum of Atlanta.

ISBN: 979-8-218-12797-8
Library of Congress Control Number: 2023917260

This is a work of nonfiction, and every attempt was made by the author to get the "facts" straight unless noted otherwise. But when I think about memoirs of this nature, I am reminded of the quote from longtime columnist Jimmy Breslin, who, in *Can't Anybody Here Play This Game?* his book about the 1962 New York Mets, wrote, "Most legends should be regarded with suspicion. Although if one is to have any fun out of life, one should proceed with the understanding that reminiscences are to be enjoyed not authenticated."

Published October 2023
© 2023, Murray Browne

In memory of my father

Your memory is a monster; you forget—it doesn't. It simply files things away. It keeps things for you or hides things from you—and summons them to your recall with a will of its own. You think you have a memory; but it has you!

—John Irving, *A Prayer for Owen Meany*

Every man's death begins with the death of his father.

—Orhan Pamuk, *My Father*

I have this huge archive of unreleased material. It's enormous. And I've started listening to things again, some of these pieces are 20 or 30 years old. I've started hearing them in a different way. So, one of the things I've been doing here is taking pieces from the archive and actually working on them further. Suddenly diving back into a piece that I'd completely forgotten about from 16 years ago or something like that. It's so unfamiliar, like a piece by another person. So, I feel I'm sort of collaborating with my various old selves. These sort of enthusiastic strangers who walk into the studio from 1995 or something like that.

Lindsay Zoladz, "Designing Music to Create a Mood" *New York Times*, November 8, 2020 (Interview with Brian Eno during the pandemic)

Table of Contents

PREFACE

Anyone who has the luxury of being able to retire (and it is a luxury because oftentimes it is dependent on health and wealth) needs a project. What you are holding in your hand is one of those projects, but it did take some time to get here.

The journey began in the spring of 2019 after twelve years of employment at a multimedia company based in Atlanta, when I received an email notification from the parent corporation that I was eligible for a generous one-year severance package to leave the company. The timetable was such that it would take me right up to my sixty-fifth birthday and Medicare eligibility. My initial reaction was shock. I yelled to myself, "I don't think I have to work anymore!" I had been working steadily for forty-five years at a series of jobs (you wouldn't call it a career) with little love for work—a trait you will later understand was part of my upbringing.

The feelings of disbelief were reminiscent to those I had when the Chicago Cubs won the World Series in 2016. I grew up in rural East Central Illinois listening to the Cubs on the radio in the afternoons or catching them occasionally on television. (My baptism of disappointment was the 1969 collapse to the New York Mets.) But on that November night in Cleveland, when the grinning Kris Bryant threw across the diamond to first baseman Anthony Rizzo for the final out, decades of frustration evaporated. That 2019 corporate email felt exactly like that. I was in shock for a moment, before throwing the equivalent of a baseball mitt in the air and looking around for loved ones to hug.

I hugged my longtime partner, Denise Casey, and she was as elated as I was. She had retired a few years earlier, and I promised her that if I ever got a package, we'd take a long trip to Europe. I kept my word, and we visited Italy, Prague, Slovenia, and Berlin, where my older daughter, Cynthia, lived. When I returned, I was a little nervous about my future even though my financial planner confirmed that I had the resources to retire.

Still, I went to the career counseling service provided by my former employer, where I was surrounded by people who were more dedicated to finding a job than I was. Resume writing, mastering the intricacies of LinkedIn, recommitting to the power of networking, and polishing my personal brand were all part of the curriculum. I write about the experience in more detail in Chapter 5, but my initial takeaway was the confirmation that I didn't like managing people or large projects or sitting in meetings and pretending to be interested. (One of the skills in making it to retirement is not to slough off or appear that you are mailing it in.[1]) So when people asked me what I got from outplacement training, my reply was "I realized that I don't want to work anymore," which is kind of funny though it shouldn't have surprised anyone who knew me well.

Retirement provided the time to allow the toxins of work to flush out of my system and to reflect on what I wanted to do in my post-work era. Fortunately, a trailblazer was already in our household. As mentioned, my partner, Denise, had already retired and, out of respect for me, had controlled her daily bliss as I trudged off to work. To keep my morale up, she prepared delicious evening meals that I could smell as soon as I opened the front door. We called it the Lucky Bastard Café. (Such is the language of lovers.) This still left plenty of time for her to pursue her own interests as well, including travel, reading, and sewing. The latter activity connected her to cherished times when she sewed with her late mother. Denise coined our new mantra: "In retirement, everyone needs a project."

---

1   As a word of advice, you shouldn't even talk about retirement or aging if you're trying to stay employed in your later years. Avoid saying things like "Every time the weather changes, my knees hurt," or "Back in 2009, we did it this way," or "Why do I care? I probably won't be here in a couple of years." This is the kind of talk that will be remembered when upper management is thinking of thinning the ranks. Other bad ideas for older employees include accepting mylar balloons wishing you a happy sixtieth birthday delivered to your office cube or wallpapering your cube with pictures of grandchildren, as cute as they might be.

CHAPTER 1: LETTERS AS ARTIFACTS

Am I part of the last generation that even wrote letters? I say this with trepidation because we baby boomers always think we are special at everything. As I cleaned out my closet, I was surprised to unearth many letters from my lifelong friends with whom I exchanged correspondence. We still keep in touch regularly, but by the late 1980s, those letters had become a trickle as we shifted to email.

Nowadays, these same emails-as-correspondence seem quite quaint, and unless you had the foresight to print them—like some old-timey corporate president who had his secretary filter and print everything—these electronic letters have mostly disappeared into the digital ether unless, perhaps, you have been the focus of a subpoena. Texts, Twitter, and social media have eclipsed email for keeping in touch. If I really want to connect, I phone friends and family because it allows for bantering back and forth. A handwritten letter, even one written on a computer and printed, has a special meaning to those who understand letters. Part of that added meaning is the time it takes to find a stamp, address the envelope, and carry it to the nearest mailbox. To many, letters have become the provenance of history museums.

For example, I have a framed Civil War letter from my grandmother's uncle Henry Kelley that hangs in my study. Written on November 30, 1863, from a field hospital after the Battle of Missionary Ridge, the letter begins:

> Dear Father:
>
> It is with pleasure that I take my pen in hand to inform you of my condition. I was in fight on the 15th at Mission Ridge and was wounded in the left hip slightly it did not injure any bones. I was able to set up all the time and walk about and getting along fine. [Uncle Henry did not recover from his wound and later died of gangrene.]

In addition to its preservation under glass, this letter is still readable because in the past, even people of modest education often had much better penmanship. Proper cursive handwriting was doubtless imprinted by repeated drilling into our hand's muscle memory. Cursive writing, reportedly faster than printing, is no longer taught in schools, though my older daughter, Cynthia, still writes in a sort of cursive scrawl. My younger daughter, Bonnie, does not. Denise, who came through a Catholic school system, shudders when recalling the nuns' strict adherence to proper handwriting. Is there a connection between Catholicism and cursive handwriting? Perhaps. Recently, when I complimented the graying receptionist at my periodontist's office about her crisp handwriting on my appointment card, she muttered, "Catholic schools."

The letter, like a conventional photograph, requires no special equipment to view its contents unlike a VCR tape, a reel-to-reel audio tape, or a digital photograph. Judith Schalansky in the Preface to *An Inventory of Losses* says it best:

> Sometimes I imagine the future thus: generations to come standing baffled in today's data storage media, strange aluminum boxes whose contents, owing to rapid advances in platforms and programming languages and file formats, and playback devices, have become nothing but meaningless codes, and moreover ones

that, as an object in themselves, exude less of an aura than the knots of an Inca quipu string, as eloquent as they are mute, or those mystifying ancient Egyptian obelisks that may commemorate triumph and tragedy, no one knows.

And it's not just the words. The paper itself, and any letterhead or preprinted image, adds meaning to the artifact. In the framed Civil War letter, stationery must have been readily available to the soldiers writing home. There is a short single-panel cartoon that graces the letter. While in formation, eight Union soldiers break rank by glancing over their left shoulders. The officer in front of them yells "*Front face! Why in thunder don't you cast your eyes to the front?*"

The officer doesn't see that behind the formation is a belle in full dress, lifting her petticoat slightly to reveal a seductive ankle and mid-calf. A light military moment obfuscates the grim news of the letter.

Letters from my friends were often written on the backs of office memos and lab reports, indicating frugality or that the letter was composed during work hours. Either way, they provided an unintentional glimpse of their work lives. A few coffee stains only added to a letter's veracity.

THE LETTERS

The letters of my father, Glenn R. Browne Jr. (1925–1985) cover two important periods of his life. The first set of about two hundred letters were written to his parents, Glenn Reginald Browne and Forrest Murray Browne, while he was in the service; they included combat action in France and Germany during the winter of 1944–1945.

The second set of two hundred letters covered a brief period in the fall of 1976 and then from 1980 until his death from leukemia in March 1985. These were written to me. I do recall that he wrote to me regularly while I was a student at Indiana University from 1973 to 1976. Regretfully, those letters were either lost or destroyed. For this mistake, I blame my youth.

Why no letters from 1977 to 1979? I was living relatively close to home then,[2] and my father felt my proximity didn't merit a letter. Another example of how time and distance factor in adding significance to any letter written. My grandmother handed me the war letters before she died, and they stayed in a plastic box for three decades.

The second set was in an unmarked cardboard box in my closet. Included in the second set was the last letter he wrote me before his death. The letters were like personal time capsules. I knew someday I would have to exhume them.

But letters were not enough to fill out his narrative. Specifically, I needed more information. For my father's military experience, I consulted several WWII history books. I also referred to my father's regimental history, which sat untouched, adjacent to the World Book Encyclopedias in our Ethan Allan bookcases. After we closed the family home in the late 1980s, the book remained with his belongings until I used it to verify the whereabouts of his unit. Other books supplied more background for the narrative as well.

For his life at home, I relied more on family photos, newspaper clips, and internet searches to match events to dates. (For instance, if my dad mentioned watching Dan Marino in the Super Bowl against the San Francisco 49ers, I determined that it was January 1985.) One challenge was that he rarely dated his letters. I also drew on the memories of my family. One person who my father mentioned often was his brother, my uncle Sam. Though uncle Sam lived nearby while I was growing up, I wasn't around him much, and he has since died.

Fortunately, I have kept in touch with Sam's oldest child, my cousin Jane Carroll, who was helpful in triangulating some of those experiences since she is several years older than I.[3]

Of course, we are all relying on what have been called "unreliable memories."[4] More on this later, but without question, some details of my father's life are constructed from such memories. For example:

After Christmas dinner at my grandfather and grandmother Browne's house, we'd gather by the tree to pass out gifts. They had a modestly decorated short,

---

2   From 1977 to 1980, I lived in Danville, Illinois, and then Champaign, Illinois, before moving to Wichita, Kansas.

3   A branch of the family tree is in the Appendix A.

4   A term based on *Unreliable Memoirs*, the name of Clive James' wonderful book about growing up in Australia during World War II.

plump tree featuring large homemade gingerbread cookies. Finally, after the gifts were distributed, we began to soak the cookies in milk and devour them. Although they were hard (hardtack hard, so we'd savor them, no?), I believed them to be tasty, and they became a treasured memory of a grandmother's love. I mentioned this memory to my cousin Jane Carroll, and she shrieked, "Those cookies tasted terrible, and our grandmother ordered them from a woman in town."

This anecdote serves as a reminder that our memories cannot be treated with gospel-like reverence. In her 1995 memoir, *The Liars' Club*, a staple of the memoir canon, Mary Karr wrote about her East Texas oil town upbringing, nonchalantly noting in an interview that if the people she grew up with didn't accept her version of events, they should write their own books.

But I do have a responsibility to make this book as truthful as possible. Glenn R. Browne Jr. had four grandchildren, but the oldest, Cynthia, was only two years old when he died. Thus, none of them have any personal recollection of him. At least my dad knew that he had a future generation who might speak his name after he was gone.

Perhaps you will glean some useful wisdom from these pages. I myself was surprised to discover several reoccurring trends that have permeated my life for decades. But why should I be surprised? After all, in the words of the Czech writer Milan Kundera, we live on the planet of inexperience. He writes:

> We are born one time only, we can never start a new life equipped with the experience we've gained from the previous one. We leave childhood without knowing what youth is, we marry without knowing what it is to be married, and even when we enter old age, we don't know what it is we're heading for: the old are innocent children of their own age. In that sense, man's world is the planet of inexperience.

CHAPTER 2:
THE BATTLEFRONT MONTHS

I knew that my father had fought in World War II, but he rarely mentioned his experiences. Only after reviewing his letters from 1943 to 1946 did I begin to understand this critical time of his life.

According to family lore,[5] my father wanted to enlist soon after the war broke out, but his parents would not allow it until he finished high school. He joined the army in July 1943. First, he was sent to Kansas University in Lawrence and enrolled in the Army Specialized Training Reserve Program (ASTRP), but that program was soon terminated. Consequently, he did his basic training at Fort Benning, Georgia, and further training at Camp Van Dorn, Mississippi. He was promoted to instrument corporal, then sent to Europe in December 1944.

He ended up as the number-one gunner in a heavy machine gun platoon with

---

5   I know "family lore" is vague term, but my definition of family lore is "some family-related story I heard from someone at some time, but I cannot recall who from or verify its truth."

the 254th Infantry Regiment of the 63rd Division, which included carrying the tripod of the 30-caliber medium machine gun. On occasion, in an attempt to downplay the ferocity of the combat, he would joke that his division "broke the back of the Wehrmacht on the Siegfried Line." But the reality was that in the bitter cold of January 1945, he fought in the Alsace region of France south of Strasbourg (known as the Colmar Pocket). On March 17, 1945, his unit shifted northeast of Strasbourg, attacking the Siegfried Line near Ensheim and Kaiserslautern. These military operations may not be as well-known as other campaigns in the European Theatre, but they were no less dangerous.[6]

My grandparents saved these letters. When my grandmother died in 1988, they were passed to me and they remained untouched and unread for over thirty-five years. Did I read each letter carefully? The answer is no, but I did skim through them all.

My father wrote home to his "folks" regularly. The letters from Kansas, Georgia, and Mississippi alternated between accounts of army training life and replies to news from home from his parents. No doubt his parents living in his hometown of Hoopeston, Illinois, wrote often; my father often thanked them for "their swell letter." He signed the letters "Diddy," a nickname often used by his parents and relatives on my father's side. My father's older brother, my uncle Sam[7], gave him the name during their early childhood days. Very few others called him Diddy, and I always felt that my father did not particularly like that name. He certainly did not encourage anyone else to use the name; I cannot recall my mother ever doing so.

I was most interested in the letters from November 1944 through the summer

---

6   One reason that the Colmar Pocket doesn't receive the historical notoriety is because the heavy fighting roughly coincided with the more well-known Battle of the Bulge, Germany's last great offensive of the war. Some of the heaviest fighting was near the village of Jebsheim, a German stronghold. My father writes specifically of killing a German officer in the middle of the night at a roadblock in Jebsheim. In the same account—written decades after the war—he is somewhat matter of fact in describing everything, including names of his buddies who were wounded and killed in action.

7   More about the oddity of family names. So my uncle's name was Samuel Prescott Browne or Sam Browne for short. The "Sam Browne" belt, which was a common military belt and popular in the first half of the twentieth century, had a strap across the shoulder hooking to a waist belt worn over the uniform. (Although my uncle was only a couple of years older than my father, he was ineligible for the armed services. A childhood accident had severed all the fingers of his right hand, leaving only his thumb.) Speaking of family names, my father did not like his middle name, "Reginald," and family lore (again that term) may explain why neither I nor my older brother Neil or my younger sister Kay had middle names.

of 1945. This was when he was a combat soldier in Europe. But I tempered my expectations.

I've read a fair amount of history, including military history; one of the more influential books shaping my expectations was Gerald F. Linderman's *The World Within War: America's Combat Experience in World War II*, which I read soon after it was published in 1997. Linderman studied the relationships war veterans had "with their enemies, their comrades, their commanders, and even their families." The basic premise of the book was that combat veterans in World War II kept much of their experience to themselves.

Linderman writes in his introduction:

> Letters from soldiers to their families were multitudinous, but the writers ordinarily chose assurance over realism. Besides, cultural constraints, notably the American veneration of individualism and self-sufficiency, made it difficult for soldiers to own to their loneliness and vulnerability.

My father's letters to my grandparents while he was on the front lines in France and Germany were short and vague. There may have been two factors at play here. One is that soldiers knew that troop movements would be censored. And secondly, they may have been following Linderman's theme of frontline soldiers keeping their emotions buttoned up to reassure loved ones.

For example, on December 24, 1944, soon after arriving in France, my father wrote home:

> Folks,
>
> I know it's useless to say not to worry, because you will, but remember it won't do me any good and it bothers me to know you are worrying. This business is harder on the people who are left at home waiting. I have one of the safest jobs in the outfit. (I stay with the CO of the outfit and we are supporting and bring up the guns when needed.) Be thankful I'm not a rifleman or on the guns. Don't worry about me doing anything that is not in the line of duty.

Another reason the letters were short was the use of V-mail, a technology developed in the late 1930s. Correspondence was limited to one page, which was photographed on microfilm. The exposed film was sent back to the States and developed, and a small photographic print (just over 4 x 5 inches) was mailed to the addressee. One interesting aspect is that, unlike paper letters,

V-mail correspondence has survived rather well. As with paper letters, sensitive information, such as locations or descriptions of any military action, was censored.

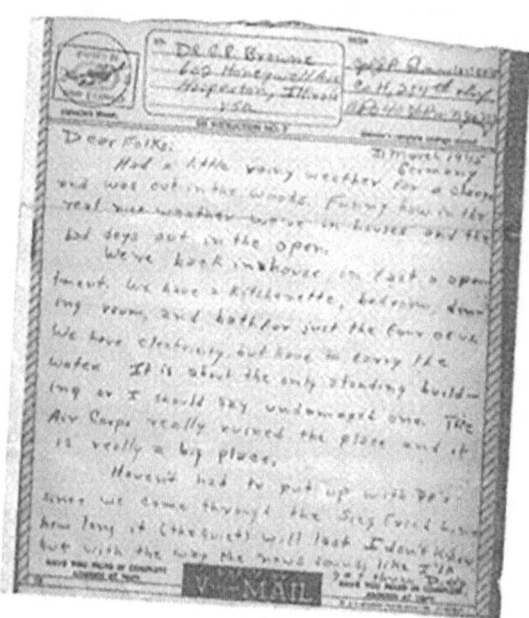

Common in the letters were complaints about the cold and rain. This is understandable, given that the European winter of 1944–1945 was one of the coldest and wettest on record. Possibly this contributed to my father's longtime hatred of the cold—for years, he was deaf to my mother's requests to air-condition the house. And once he special-ordered a pickup truck to avoid the standard factory air-conditioning.

Because my father's battlefront correspondence for the nearly three months from January until late March 1945 lacked details for the aforementioned reasons, I relied on several other sources to triangulate his whereabouts.

Rick Atkinson's monumental *The Guns at Last Light: The War in Western Europe, 1944–45*, the third volume of the Liberation Trilogy, was most helpful. Atkinson is a masterful storyteller and, thus, one of my favorite historians. His attention to detail is most impressive. While on his book tour in 2013 for *The Guns at Last Light*, Atkinson graciously (and patiently) fielded questions in the library auditorium from audience members who asked about their fathers who fought in the war.[8] (It was like a parlor game in which everyone tried to stump him, but no one could.) Atkinson's book provided a detailed overview of the action in the Colmar Pocket and the breakthrough of the southern part of the Siegfried Line. Another important source was the uncopyrighted

---

8   Denise and I met Atkinson afterwards to get our book signed; he wrote "In memory of your fathers Glenn Browne and Mickey Koslow." Denise's father was with the 97th Bombardment Group in North Africa and Italy. (Previously, when Atkinson toured for his second book of the trilogy on the war in Italy, *The Day of Battle*, he signed a book for Mickey, who was still alive then, "Thank you for your service.")

regimental history of the 254th Infantry of the 63rd Division.[9] This slim, now-faded booklet was compiled by the regiment after the war. While the book has a factual, sanitized tone, it lacks some of the niceties like maps and timelines.

In addition to these historical sources and V-mail, I used a long, four-page letter my father wrote to his parents dated April 25, 1944, as the war in Europe was winding down. It included a map of the attack on the Siegfried Line and his candid account, including being shelled while he was in the village of Ensheim on March 17, 1944. I am not convinced this letter was ever mailed as it was written on conventional stationery. My guess is that he wrote it but never sent it and simply carried it home. The photo of him was taken at Kaiserslautern, a few miles beyond the Siegfried Line, in March 1945.[10] It was also during this brief but intense period in the war that Corporal Glenn R. Browne was awarded the Bronze Star for leading his unit to safety after they were pinned down by enemy fire. [11]

ADDING PERSPECTIVE

My father rarely talked about his war experiences. Only later in life did he go to any army reunions, though he did write occasionally to former comrades. There was also a large framed panoramic photo of his unit that hung (proudly, I assume) over the freezer in our utility room for years. I have no idea what happened to it.

Once my grandmother commented that my father was a different person

9   Oddly enough, the 63rd Division is not mentioned in Atkinson's account of the action, which at first confused me. I later found on the internet that the 63rd was temporarily placed under the more well-known 3rd Division in the campaign, and some units were briefly folded into the 100th Division. Lieutenant Audie Murphy, who later became a movie star in Westerns, was in the 3rd Division and earned his Medal of Honor as a nineteen-year- old holding off a German counterattack by himself in the Colmar Pocket. Linderman includes passages about Murphy's view of combat in his book as well.

10   The longer, non-V-mail letters that my father wrote home in the summer of 1945 also revealed his experiences. These letters were more informative and gruffer in tone. He mentioned seeing displaced persons on trains back to Holland and bombed-out cities, but he had little sympathy for the German civilians in general. He even complained about the Red Cross in a letter dated July 29, 1945, using Red Cross stationery. He wrote: "Have a thing to say about the Red Cross they are getting worse, all the time. Charge 20 cents for a meal that wouldn't fill my hollow tooth. The same with coffee and doughnuts.   P.S. Nice guy me—panning the Red Cross on their stationery." Linderman mentions the same complaint from soldiers about being charged for coffee and donuts in his book.

11   With the exception of the certificate accompanying his medal, I did not learn any of the specifics of his heroism.

when he came home, but she never elaborated.

As a child, my favorite toys were the Marx military playsets sold through the Sears and Roebuck catalogs. Today I wonder what he must have thought watching me playing with them—which I did, constantly, on the floor of the family room near his favorite easy chair. He never said anything. Possibly, it did not bother him because it was he who bought me my first WWII army set for Christmas. I played with them for hundreds of hours. Later, I added German and Japanese soldiers as well, but the American soldiers always won.

Another complexity in understanding his attitude about war was that my father read a fair amount of military history. His favorite book was Alistair Horne's *The Price of Glory* about Verdun in World War I. He even made a detailed map, including marking the French forts, which I later found in his things. Years later, I finally read Horne's excellent Verdun book and two other of his works—*A Savage War of Peace: Algeria 1954–1962* and *Hubris: The Tragedy of War in the Twentieth Century*. My father also liked the Ballantine *Illustrated History of World War II* series, which focused on various battles and the specifics of military aircraft like the German ME-109 Messerschmidt and the British Spitfire. He had a lifelong interest in aircraft, building model airplanes from balsa-wood kits as a youth. My grandmother remarked that making models ruined his eyes because he did not have adequate light.

As I was growing up, Dad made World War II model planes from plastic kits. He would then hang his finished pieces—a Messerschmidt, a Japanese Zero, a Spitfire— in air combat poses with invisible nylon thread from the ceiling of the bedroom I shared with my brother. They were exquisitely painted and decaled without a smudge. I tried making them, too, but lost interest soon after accidentally squirting a gob of airplane glue in my eye.

He did make it clear that while he was opposed to the waste of the Vietnam war (he was worried that my older brother would be drafted), he did not like the campus protests. If he had lived longer, I am not sure I would have asked about his war experiences, but we probably would have talked about the Horne books and the Atkinson Liberation Trilogy.[12]

---

12   Denise's father read the first two Atkinson books before he died, and when she called him daily on her drive to work, he would go on and on about them. It makes sense. For those at the front or directly engaged with troop support, the world is limited to fighting, surviving, and the daily hardships of military life. Books like Atkinson's *Liberation Trilogy* gave Denise's father a glimpse of the big picture and a better understanding of what was going on in the entire theatre of warfare, whether it be North Africa, Italy, or Western Europe.

CHAPTER 3: THE HOMEFRONT YEARS

There is another set of letters from my father. While I did not save all of them, the ones I did are from 1973 (when I began college at Indiana University) to just before his death in 1985. Most of the earliest letters from this time have been lost. Dad didn't like to talk on the telephone, so most of my regular collect calls home were for Mom. Dad would say hello and but not much else, sometimes remarking, "If I talk, I won't have anything to write about." Nonetheless, I hung on to his letters after graduating from college in 1976, perhaps with the same fortitude that my grandparents held on to their son's war letters.

Despite what might seem dull subject matter (and you might be correct), I now see that buried in the minutiae of these letters were flashes of insight, including thoughts about the world of work, his children (including me), and somewhat oblique observations about business and life. All this was hiding within his recitations of the weather, televised football games (I did not realize he was such a fan of the pigskin), animal stories (including his battle with insects in the garden[13]), and automotive repairs. (He had an affinity for the Chevrolet Vega, a 1970s era subcompact that became known for its wide range of problems, ranging from rust to reliability.)

You could not bullshit my father. He once remarked that he would have made a good lawyer because he could see the fallacies of other people's statements, but he was not a lawyer. Rather, he was an accountant who worked for the Milford Canning Company[14] for over thirty years, despite his MBA from the prestigious University of Chicago, where George Schultz was one of his professors. Schultz would go on to serve as secretary of labor under President Richard Nixon and secretary of state under Ronald Reagan.

While taking a photography class in my senior year of college, I took this photo of Dad watering his dog Charlie that opens this chapter about life on the home front. The filthy, ungroomed mongrel in the photo was a purebred Welsh terrier but never resembled a show dog. My mother did a lot of research in picking this breed to replace our family mutt Pepper, but Charlie was always in touch with his grimy miner heritage. Charlie just tolerated Mom. In contrast, he was a constant companion to my father as he worked daily on our two acres of yard and garden. We lived just outside the city limits, and Charlie would sometimes disappear to a nearby drainage ditch/creek to "chase rat" (Dad's all-encompassing classification for opossums, groundhogs, and large rodents). This is a characteristic of Welsh terriers. You cannot see Dad's face here, but these are the times in the yard I think he was most content. I don't believe that Dad expected happiness, nor did he think much about it. The matter-of-fact tone of his letters contains not a hint of drama.

LETTERS AS PRIMARY SOURCES

When I first received them, it never occurred to me to consider these letters "historical documents" or "primary sources" and certainly not a time capsule illustrating the mindset of a Midwesterner circa 1975–1985. But, in fact, they

---

13   His battle with insects escalated to the point that he realized he had overdone it once when there were no honeybees around.

14   See Milford, Illinois map in the Appendix B.

are all these things. I can honestly say that I am now the only person alive who can interpret them. Obviously, Dad didn't think of them as any of these things either. And as he rarely dated the letters, I was only able to date them by recalling my own history. What often helped is that he would photocopy cartoons on one side and then type his letter on the other.

Cartoons were typically dated by month and day but not by year, so they could help pinpoint the approximate time of year. Photocopiers in this era didn't make crisp copies, and the copies had a chemical feel to them, but they've held up well, like the V-mails from the war. Dad typed these letters at work, with minimal editing. Typos, Wite-Out corrections, and scratch outs were included; this gives them a rawness matching whatever Dad had on his mind at the time. Also, as I see it now, there's an underlying "fucking off while at work" message that gives the letters a somewhat subversive tone, which I enjoy.

CARTOONISH

One element included in almost all his letters was the cartoons clipped from newspapers. Since his letters were single spaced and one page, each week Dad created his own personal stationery by photocopying a set of his favorite cartoons onto one page and then typing the letter on the other side.

The cartoons ranged from *Frank and Ernests* and editorial cartoons from the *Chicago Tribune* to an occasional *Broom-Hilda* and the dark comedy of Charles Rodrigues, who drew single-panel scatological cartoons for *Playboy* and *National Lampoon* magazines.[15]

Dad also liked to cut out cartoon figures and paste them on the outsides of envelopes. These were often on old envelopes with outdated return addresses and such. His theory about the cartoon on the envelope was that the postal workers appreciated the humor and thus would expedite his correspondence. He also would cut out Doonesbury cartoons and send them along. He especially liked the character Zonker Harris, and many salutations in the letters to me were affectionally made out to "Zonker" in quotes.

Another cartoon-based salutation that he addressed me with was "Malcolm" or "Malcolm Frazzle," the protagonist of Mark Alan Stamaty's strip, *MacDoodle St.*, which first appeared in the *Village Voice* and was later collected in a 1980 book that I shared with Dad. Set in the bustling, chaotic streets of New York City, the poet Frazzle works as a dishwasher and contributes his poems to

---

15   Rodrigues's more "acceptable" work was syndicated in the *Chicago Tribune*.

Dishwasher's Monthly. Eventually, Frazzle is called upon to save the world from an evil corporation that has developed a breed of dishwashing monkeys. But Malcolm is doubtful as he couldn't even fix a washing machine:[16]

On the surface, this is funny, but for us, it had additional meaning. While Dad was a great home repair man[17], I had neither the aptitude for fixing things nor the inclination to learn. My experiences working with him were limited to being an "extra pair of hands." I don't think he was disappointed in me, but I recall Mom telling me to get out there in the garage with him and learn something.

But Dad did mention this comic to me in one of his letters. He wrote, "While I enjoy Malcolm very much— solving the world's problems permits simplistic solutions and moral issues but fixing a refrigerator requires ability." Cementing this connection, I gave him a cheap plastic combination calculator and ruler inscribed with "Dishwasher's Monthly." He raved about how much he liked it[18] and often referred to his weekly letters as the latest edition of *Dishwasher's Monthly*.

There were several cartoons that Dad sent that followed me throughout my life. To me, they transcended humor as aphorisms of wisdom and have remained memorable. One is from Frank Cotham, a notable cartoonist for *The New Yorker*, which strikes me as odd because I don't remember Dad reading that magazine.

---

16   Excerpted from the graphic novel *MacDoodle St.*, NY Review Comics, ©1978 and 2019 Mark Alan Stamaty. Reprinted with permission.

17   He even dreamed about repairs. He admitted that he had a Walter Mitty fantasy of being an international super repairman who could be sent to Buckingham Palace to fix the queen's clogged sink.

18   Parents! They can be so grateful for so little!

I stapled this cartoon to a piece of cardboard and put it in a cheap frame (for preservation?) because the message was clear: don't act like a loser because people will treat you like a loser. Good advice, perhaps, but I don't think Dad intended it as a special message because he sent hundreds of cartoons during those years. I remind myself and others of this quote whenever I hear someone I care about putting themselves down. I even add my own take: "No need to put yourself down because there are plenty of others willing to do that for you."

Cotham

"I'm sorry I kicked you, but when I saw you were a loser, I couldn't resist it."

www.cartoonstock.com

Another cartoon came from the *Wall Street Journal* and appeared on the back of a letter Dad wrote in September 1982. Again, there was no special references to the Bob Schochet cartoon in the letter, but the joke also touches on the topic of self-pity. In the cartoon, a maintenance worker is standing in front of the large desk of the company president. The maintenance worker says, "If it makes you feel any better, it's lonely at the bottom too."

ORGANIZING THE LETTERS

Judith Schalansky writes in *An Inventory of Losses* that chronology "is the most unoriginal of all the organizational principles, being only a simulation of order." This quote comforts me. Most of Dad's letters were undated; I didn't have the forethought to store them in their postmarked envelopes. Thus, as I reread them, I made a conscious editorial decision to look for emerging patterns and to organize the letters by topic, not chronology.

WORK

Simply put, the greatest pain in the ass in his daily life was the world of work.

The timeline around 1951 when Dad began his professional career remains a little fuzzy to me. My father officially graduated from The Citadel, the Military College of South Carolina, in 1951 (part of the GI Bill), and he was married in January 1951. During this time, he was already working at the Milford Canning Company in our hometown—perhaps in between semesters. For as long as I can remember, he was treasurer of the Milford Canning Company. With an MBA from the University of Chicago, he now seems to me to have been clearly overqualified. And it remains a mystery why he worked there for decades.

In addition to his financial duties, my father represented the company in its occasional battles with various environmental entities. He regularly represented the company during negotiations with the union and the Migrant Council, which represented the hundreds of migrants who came to the area from the Texas-Mexico border to work in the fields and factories in the spring and summer.[19]

My grandfather was once a partial owner of the Milford Canning Company but later sold his interest in the company to a man named Smith, who took pride in his resemblance to the folksinger/entertainer Burl Ives. Dad did not like Smith. For this reason, my siblings and I were never allowed to watch the 1964 television version of *Rudolph the Red-Nosed Reindeer* or listen to Christmas standards sung by Ives. He also disliked the son, Smith Jr., who later took my father's office and moved Dad's desk to a small cubicle near the hallway.

Sometime in the early 1970s, Dad and my uncle Sam went on strike. This was not some wildcat walkout affair but a calculated coup. Here's the setup:

---

19   When I was growing up in Milford in the 1960s and 1970s, these migrant workers were simply referred to by the locals as "migrants" or "the Mexicans." Looking back, I understand it was wrong to collectively label this diverse group as one people.

each year, the Harris Bank in Chicago loaned the Milford Canning Company the money required to run corn pack in the late summer when the corn was harvested and canned over six weeks. After the canned goods were sold, the bank would be repaid. Unlike in previous seasons, this time around, my father and uncle worked with outside legal counsel to draw up an ironclad contract. This contract renegotiated their salaries, their bonuses, and the conditions of their employment. They presented this new contract to the Smiths before the Harris Bank loan was approved for the upcoming harvest season.

As expected, the Smiths initially refused to sign, but then they did. What prompted them to do so was simply that Harris Bank would not float the traditional seasonal loan to the Milford Canning Company if Dad and my uncle Sam were not the company officers.

It was tense at our house for a week or two, but the Smiths soon capitulated. After signing the contract, they could not terminate my father's employment without a big payout. Nonetheless, they did try to make his life miserable in the hopes that he would simply leave the company.

Eventually, the Smiths sold Milford Canning to Fremont[20], a corporation that had consolidated formerly independent canning companies—the most notable being a sauerkraut company in Wisconsin. Later, my uncle Sam left Milford and moved to Ohio to work at the corporate headquarters in Fremont, leaving my father to manage the affairs of my grandparents.

Even though my father worked for a small company in a small town, he had his theories about corporations. And he regularly shared these in his letters. He read *The Wall Street Journal* and *The Chicago Tribune* daily (and not just for the cartoons that he religiously clipped).

Now, let us review his thoughts.

THE CANNING BUSINESS MODEL

Dad wrote in one letter:

> Ninety days after I started at Milford nearly thirty- three years ago, I realized I hadn't found the Lost Dutchman mine and that canning was not the path to wealth. Seasonal canning represents a one-inventory-a year turnover, and it was to each individual company's advantage to unload the inventory as fast as possible. The buyers

---

20   According to their website, they are still makers of tomato-based sauces and pickled vegetables.

are larger and few in numbers and exert a great deal of pressure while the canner is seasonal or otherwise needs sales to continue production. Canners have worshipped the phrase "People got to eat." And hoped for the day they were the suppliers, and the only suppliers, so they would get their price revenge.

To set all this in geographic context, consider this: in Milford, billboards proudly announced that Milford was "The Buckle on the Corn Belt" and nearby Hoopeston was "The Sweet Corn Capital of the World." Later, his letters would chronicle the demise of the once-thriving canning industry as area factories closed or consolidated.

ENVIRONMENTAL CONCERNS

If you haven't spent much time near large farming or food-processing operations, it might not occur to you that such operations can be significant polluters. Such pollution can range from mild (bad smells) to severe (illness or death from bacterial or chemical pollutants).[21]

Dad represented the company before Milford's board of trustees on issues that included both nuisance odors and more serious pollution concerns. For many years, the company filled several lagoons with wastewater from washing the corn before canning. For quicker evaporation, the fermenting wastewater of the lagoons was pumped by large sprayers to nearby fields outside town, including several behind our house.

There was a joke about Milford Canning in our high school yearbook. I clearly remember the caption under a photo of the village's welcome sign: "Milford, the Buckle on the Smell Belt." My mother took offense; she understood this was exactly the type of criticism my father had to defend against on behalf of the company. Additionally, farming and canning were the economic engines of the local economy. Representing the company was one of my dad's least favorite duties. He observed that:

> Their veiled threat to act on odor complaints at the Company upset me at first, but in the light of all other problems, a trivial manner. When I rode into Milford 34 years ago, it smelled, and it still does and if we would leave tomorrow, they would find a

---

21   By today's standards, these farming and food production operations were relatively small. When I was growing up, the smell was a constant problem, but many livelihoods depended on it. I cannot speak to the long-term effects of the pollution, but I wouldn't deny they exist.

monstrous junkyard and a large cattle feeding operation at the South city limits.[22]

One lamebrained idea concocted by the then-owners, the pipe-smoking Smith and his son, tasked my father with investigating the possibilities of selling the huge piles of factory-discarded corncobs to a corncob pipe company. (The owner must have been inspired by the pipe-smoking Burl Ives.)

BUSINESS ADMINISTRATION AND ACCOUNTING

As early as October 1976, my father wrote to me about Milford Canning's financials. This included a discussion of sales-to-working-capital ratio and this quote: "Business admin is the way the world should be, and accounting tells the world how it really is."

One time I suggested to Dad that he should teach accounting. His reply was that he simply wasn't qualified—he had never seen black ink in all his years at the company, just the red ink of financial loss.[23]

UNIONS

As much as he disliked it, my father represented the company in its negotiations with the union. One consolation was that the union leaders confided that they knew Dad wouldn't posture or bullshit them; it just wasn't his nature to do so. He wrote in one letter:

> Will start preliminary union negotiating this Friday and the problem will be how to share nothing with them. The last time I made a mistake of trying to talk and waiting to find out what Sam wanted. [Uncle Sam was by then a COO type with the Fremont corporation]. What ended up giving up, I wouldn't have any problem with, so I just won't discuss it with him. On top of that we spent big bucks on an attorney from Ohio, who thought he was a Larry Hagman[24] look alike."

22   My father was referring to a second cattle operation that was not part of Milford Canning.

23   The company always operated in tenuous circumstances, in part because of the free spending for what were classified as "business" trips for the top executives. The quote about the relationship between business administration and accounting came from one of his letters, but I'm not sure whether it originated with him or not.

24   Hagman was the star of the *I Dream of Jeannie* sitcom and later was the infamous J.R. on *Dallas*.

One irony was that there was clearly a conflict of interest. While Dad represented the company in union negotiations, Mom was a union member, employed as an office receptionist and payroll clerk. Any negotiated pay increase would directly benefit our household. At the end of one letter, my father wrote:

> Not much of a letter, but I wasn't too well organized as I am working on keeping bread out of the mouth of the union during current negotiations. Would like to see the union win all their demands so that your mother could move into the upper tax bracket, but I'm afraid that MCC [Milford Canning Company] can't afford all of these goodies.

In one letter, written during a massive layoff that proved to be permanent when the company stopped packing corn, he summarized his thoughts about the union.

> The union is really a service business, and now it is the time for them [the workers] to find out. Without the union, we would have a more efficient work force, but without a union a lot of them would have lost their job through the years because someone didn't like them.

FRUGALITY AND GENEROSITY

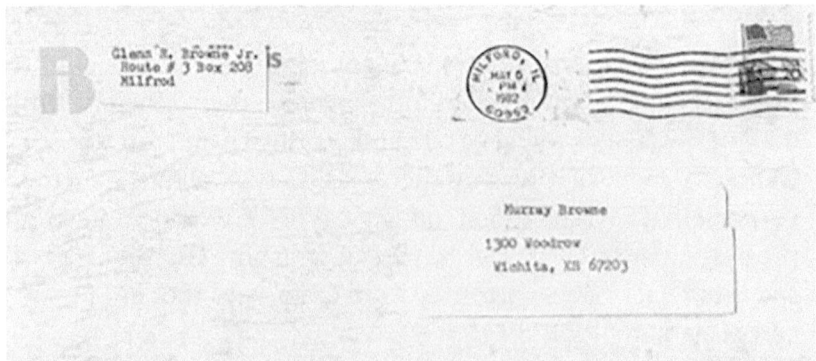

Paradoxically, Dad was both frugal and generous. And his letters reflect this. He often boasted of his thrift and his ability to uncover a good deal:

> I bought a Cricket lighter for Kay, so I could get some free Bic pens with the coupon.

> Went to Hoopeston Sunday bought 8 cartons of Kleenex @ 50

cents at Gibson's [a local precursor to Dollar General].

Sunday, we went big in the commodity market and went bullish on paper products at Ayr-Way [a precursor to Walmart]. Never done this before, but Jean and I go separate carts to double our pleasure. Was kind of fun and real savings on the name products we use. Used some of my coupons and now if the mfgs [manufacturers] have a mail-in program, I should be able to drive P & G [Proctor and Gamble] to the wall.

I know what I want for Xmas. Penney's has a short, telescoping handled umbrella for $10 (in their winter catalog—probably higher in the store unless it goes on sale, which it should before Xmas).

Perhaps this makes sense. Dad grew up during the Great Depression. And it explains why he repurposed stationery and envelopes. Many of his letters arrived in light-blue Bank of Illinois envelopes with stickers over the printed return address and addressee windows. [25] One letter he typed completely in red. "Might as well use up the red part of the ribbon," he explained.

But rarely did he scold us for wasting money, though one time he chastised me for spending forty cents on some piano sheet music ("Over the Waves") that was below my musical skill level. To this day, I recall him remarking that it took a migrant worker an hour picking asparagus to earn forty cents.

And let's not forget that this was a man who bought *three* Chevrolet Vegas.[26]

Dad's letters mentioned small checks that he sometimes sent for minor expenses. Such expenses might include the drive from Wichita, Kansas, to Illinois. He was generous in other ways, such as when he drove from Milford to Champaign, where my brother and his new wife were setting up their jewelry store, and took them out to some of the nicer chain restaurants. Dad liked to eat. He really did appreciate a good bucket of chicken or a dinner at the Elks Lodge. The cost of the meal, of course, always factored into his review. His

---

25   One letter in particular boasts that his contact at the Bank of Illinois sent him "500 defective envelopes as they were partially or completely sealed."

26   Originally, Dad bought a hunter-green Vega station wagon with a stick shift (#1). He gave it to my sister and bought himself a blue Vega station wagon—an automatic with faux wood panels (#2). The engine blew on the hunter-green station wagon, so he bought a used silver Vega coupe (#3) that was completely rusted out but only had 14K on the motor. He had the engine pulled on the coupe and installed in the original hunter-green station wagon. Of course, am I one to judge? I purchased back-to-back PT Cruisers, a poor man's version of a "statement" car.

favorite restaurant of all time was Bob Evans; his trips to see Kay in Cincinnati would always include a stop by the Bob Evans in Indianapolis. It was considered a very successful trip if he could stop in both coming and going. He called it a "two bagger."

HARD WINTERS

Many of his letters included weather reports. Bad winters or other hardships were especially concerning for his vegetable garden. Though I grew up with such winters, I later moved to more temperate climes (Tennessee and Georgia). I had forgotten how endless those gray days were with the sun going down before five. Reading these accounts returned me to my youth:

> A little freezing rain and snow this afternoon as winter has been trying to make a go of it. [We] have been creating records this October and November for below temperatures.

> Suppose to have a high in the 60s today and I don't think it busted 40 and has been overcast. The weather is like my budget—a trip into the future. For some damn unknown reason my budget is supposed to be accurate, while they seem to accept the fact that the weatherman doesn't know his nimbus from his cirrus.

ROAD TRIPS

In the early 1980s, Dad and Mom made many trips to Cincinnati and Champaign, Illinois. My sister Kay, newly divorced after being married before she was twenty, had moved to Cincinnati and was working for a CPA and studying for an accounting degree. She had a German shepherd named Gabe. He was a wonderful dog but for two annoying habits: attacking smaller dogs without provocation and chewing on one of his own paws (possibly owing to nerve damage in that leg). Regarding the former, Gabe was smart enough never to attack our family dog Charlie, the smaller Welsh terrier. With respect to the latter, the injured leg was something that my parents tried to remedy by taking the dog for weeks at a time and watching him closely so he wouldn't chew his paw raw. Since my sister was working, they took frequent trips to Cincy, which is easily over four hours bringing the dog back and forth.

They also were helping my older brother Neil and his wife set up their jewelry business in Champaign. In one letter, Dad wrote that on Friday, they had driven to Champaign to help my brother prepare both his quarterly and year-end tax

documents. Then, the next morning, "[W]e got up at 4 am and were on the road by 6 am. . . . [W]e made it to Kay's a little after one." On Monday, when they both returned to their regular jobs, he wrote: "Feel very superior today after pulling off a three-day jaunt in the middle of winter, with only about twenty miles of slick road between Fowler [Indiana] and Milford."
That is about 650 miles of driving over a three-day period!

THE WAR YEARS RETURN

Dad rarely talked about the war, but occasionally, the topic cropped up in his letters. He was opposed to the Vietnam War (or the War in Southeast Asia, as it is properly known now) because he felt our country had no business being there; he was also skeptical of the competency of both generals and politicians. While he wasn't sympathetic to campus rioting, he clearly understood (and was concerned) that my brother could be drafted via the lottery. He wrote, "They ran the last draft just like they do the income tax, with the result the poor went to Vietnam and better fixed went to college or Canada."

Later in the same letter, he referred to the correspondence he'd received from one of his war buddies, a man named John, who lived in San Francisco. This was the only service buddy with whom he kept in regular contact.

> I wrote John who said he had called the fellow that was wounded by the same shell burst as John. [This comrade was 18 when he was wounded and been confined to a wheelchair for 35 years in a VA hospital.] I quoted a passage from *All Quiet on the Western Front.* "It is hard to imagine a normal mind functioning daily on top of a mangled body— hospitals are what war is really like." . . . We had two platoon leaders seriously wounded and one killed as well as the Company Exec. The whole Division didn't get a major or above even scratched. They thought it was a lovely war as they lived like feudal kings and absolute authority and were on the winning side. [Next to the quote was a tiny newspaper clipping that read "In the democracy of the dead, all men at last are created equal."]

> The sickest thing on television is Reagan all choked up quoting a dying marine telling his father "It was worth it, and hell, yes, he would do it again!"

> You have to know the soldier didn't know he would die and probably didn't know he was wounded by his own plane.

And this from the fall of 1984, just months before Dad died:

> In the mall bookstore, they had a Ballantine War Book (paperback) on the 106th Golden Lion Industry Division and its destruction in the Battle of the Bulge (went to high school with a guy in the 106th and he was captured—we would ride around in his 4-door Model A sedan).

THE FAMILY

Often Dad would detail the activities of my brother, sister, cousins, and uncles (particularly his brother, my uncle Sam). Although he always closed his letters with "Love, Dad," he was not an overly warm and huggable kind of guy. But he wasn't distant or cold. On the contrary, his letters indirectly revealed how important family was to him, and his actions underscored that too—he spent time and money helping all of us.[27] As I see it now, he clearly expressed his love for us in the most practical ways—constant trips to help with dogs, fixing leaky faucets, and repairing cars. (He was especially good at deicing fuel lines during our long, bitter winters.)

Rarely would he criticize my brother or sister, but sometimes, underlying dissatisfaction would surface. In November 1976, when I was living in Phoenix after graduation and working at an Earth Shoe store, my brother was struggling with his engraving business. My parents were partially underwriting the business. Dad set up an interview for my brother at Fremont's Wisconsin sauerkraut factory. And if that wasn't enough, Kay was scheduled to be married in December (she was only nineteen) in a small ceremony that neither my brother nor I would be able to attend. He wrote:

> I am grateful that you are in Phoenix at this time to give Neil moral support because American Engraving, one way or another will have to fold. With Neil, we just have to make him change. He hadn't gotten his clothes (for the interview) yet, so we are going to shop for him here.

Then, another letter a few weeks later:

> Considering how you feel or don't feel about Phoenix, it is good that you are heading home after the first of the year. I'm glad you called to let us know and I hope you get time to call your mother.

---

27   He wanted us launched! I always felt that his greatest fear was a grown child returning home.

Things aren't worse; they just aren't too much better, but if you locate nearer home and Neil does the same, it will make her feel not so lost. Should have the worry and fuss of the wedding over in a few days. . . . Had a very nice time with Kay and except for her insane driving habits. Kay hot rods it all over so with luck only the car will fall apart, and she will avoid a serious accident. Like everything in her whole life, she knows best or least is going to do it her way regardless of the possible results.

I also received advice and an occasional reprimand. When I expressed cynicism about selling shoes with my new college degree, my father hoped I would not fall into bitterness as he had. "Murray, it is bad for *me* to have a bitter and negative attitude, but I hope this doesn't become a way of life for you," he wrote.

My brother's business acumen improved, and by the early 1980s, he and his wife had a successful jewelry store in Champaign, Illinois. I believe much of their success was because of significant bookkeeping help from both my parents. But at some point, Dad realized there was a limit to his expertise and began to defer to my sister; he wrote, "Am counting on Kay to review my work."[28]

In my dad's final years, my brother had season tickets to the Illini football games, and he often invited Dad to join him, which he would often do despite the typically bad weather. "Watched three quarters of the Illinois-Missouri game and wished I watched the 4th Quarter on the 'Telly.' Neil and I stayed long enough to get soaked and then sloshed back to Jewelry Service."

But later in the season, they came better prepared. "With a camouflaged rain suit and garbage bags over my feet I was weird sight at the Illinois-Wisconsin game but a dry one."

Dad also appreciated Kay's multiple visits from Cincinnati, and she would often visit her grandparents in nearby Hoopeston as well. Anything that took the burden off him was most welcome.

And finally, he was very happy to be a grandfather. He referred to his first grandchild, Cynthia, as "Sugarfoot." Also, he made it very clear that Cynthia would be the only person allowed to call him Grandpa.

---

28   There was a little additional irony here since Dad had pushed my brother and me to take business and accounting courses while we were in college. Both of us had struggled. But he did not particularly encourage my sister, who came into the field on her own. Attitudes were changing, and it pleased Dad to have "an accountant in the family."

TIREDNESS

Dad was diagnosed with leukemia in the winter of 1983–1984. He had gone into remission by the summer, and in the fall, he retired with a full pension. Mom stayed with him every night at the Carle Clinic in Champaign, sleeping on a chair that converted to a bed. In the morning, my brother relieved my mother so she could clean up at his place and have breakfast before returning to his bedside.

This photo includes my daughter Cynthia and my sister Kay. It was in the late spring after my father's hospital stay. (That's me on the left with my Marcel Proust *In Search of Lost Time* t-shirt.) He'd lost more than 50 pounds from the chemotherapy and now resembled the 150-pound man who had been honorably discharged in 1946. He wore a ball cap the entire time because his head was cold, and you know how he hated the cold. However, he did have a beautifully shaped bald head—almost like a young bird. When his letters resumed in late 1984, most of them were written in his own hand because he was no longer going to his office and using the typewriter there. Reading his handwriting was an acquired skill as his lower-case "a" looked more like a reversed lowercase "s". The later letters expressed financial worries, specifically whether the company would pay out his pension to Mom if he died. Despite all the conflict, competition, disagreements, and resentments Dad had with his brother later in life,[29] ultimately my uncle Sam did come through for my father by securing the pension benefits for my mother.

---

29   In the early years, the two brothers were close. In fact, one of the reasons Dad went to The Citadel was to be at the same school as his older brother.

Another "very sad note" (Dad's words) in the fall of 1984 was that Charlie, the Welsh terrier, had to be put down. Mom did not really like the dog, but she knew how difficult it would be for Dad to deal with this. So she took Charlie to the vet and returned with the remains in a gunnysack. She then helped Dad bury Charlie in the back yard. Dad described, in detail, how the dog suffered with tumors, ear ruptures, open sores, and deafness and how he couldn't give Charlie any relief from his pain. I know it greatly upset him.

In early 1985, Mom and Dad went with their best friends, the Harrises, to Hawaii. For Dad, who rarely agreed to taking vacation trips, the trip to Hawaii was a way to thank my mother for her deep devotion during his hospital stay. The photos from that trip appear to be joyous, but soon after, he was sick again. Mom revealed later that he admitted he knew his cancer had returned but did not mention it while they were traveling. But if you consider they had been married for over thirty years, and given my mother's strong sense of empathy, I suspect that she already knew deep inside that he was sick again but also chose not to acknowledge it while they were traveling. In the one photograph, initially, the pair look like your typical happy Midwestern "vacationers in paradise," but their smiles are perfunctory, like Dad's embrace of Mom. The pose has more of a satisfactory "Well, we made it here" feel than one of pure bliss and relaxation. In the second photo, I feel Dad looks resigned to his fate.

THE FINAL LETTER

Before Dad went into chemotherapy again, he sent this letter on February 25, 1985. It was to be his last. Even then, he tried to be upbeat with a quick anecdote about a trip to K's Merchandise Mart, a regional chain, but later in the same letter, his tone became more serious about what was ahead for the family.

After he started chemotherapy again, not heeding his request, I visited him. He took a turn for the worse and died soon after on March 19, 1985. My brother and mother were there at his bedside. Of his last words, none seemed memorable, though he did say, "Give the axe to Murray," which did not seem significant. (At least he didn't say "Give Murray the axe.")

He also expressed regret that he did the chemo again because of the suffering and not being at home for his final days.

End of Page 1

Neil has decided to "fort up " in 'hampaign as armed robbery seems very popular. I am taking him the 25 automatic and the army 45 (am hiding the Springfield in attic under blue desk). Every once in awhile guns fail to go off due to defective ammunition so he suggested I get new ammo (the 45 stuff is 40 years old and the 25 over 20 years or more. While in K's Mdse they asked me whether it was cash or charge and I was funny and told them that I always carréd Traveler's checks in the getaway car. Really didn't leave them laughing (I also had bought 22 magnum ammo for pistol) and one scurried ± off ±kø fø to find a manager. I am glad he didn't ring alarm.

Page 2

I am glad you appreciate how I feel about coming to see me. It is a long, hard trip and there is danger in traveling. You have an obligation to your career, job, and family that properly belongs first. I know how much you care, but there is absolutely nothing you can do. I feel I will make it without the trouble of the last time as I am in real good shape and we are getting a real jump on the cancer cells as they are presently munching on platelets and not red or white cells or affecting hemogobling Jean, Neil, and Dalal will be there as a cheering section. Kay says she can't come and I am glad she finally realize the need for priorities. People resent extra work when you get sick and have nox sympathy if it is a member of the family. This is the professional approach and the way economic life is and should be.

Love,

—"Doggie Daddy"

I remember once being alone with my father in his hospital room after driving from Wichita. Reverend Larrimore,[30] our childhood minister from our hometown church, had stopped by. The reverend and I reminisced about playing basketball in the church league when I was in high school. Dad said nothing to the reverend— feigning sleep perhaps—and didn't even acknowledge his presence. When the preacher finished with a short prayer and left the room, Dad muttered, "Good man." It did not matter to the good-hearted reverend that my father was rarely seen in church. My mother always said that my father was uncomfortable in church. I can't ever remember a time when my mother forced him to attend.[31] As it happened, Reverend Larrimore spoke at my mother's funeral almost thirty years later. In preparation, I summarized my mother's beliefs with some short crib notes.[32] Despite my father's conflicted feelings about religion and the clergy, my parents were good friends with Ted and Kathy Forbes. Ted was a minister in Hoopeston, and my parents often joined the couple for dinners out or for a game of bridge. Later, the couple divorced and moved away, but both returned for my father's funeral. Ted presided over the service while Kathy sang, with haunting clarity, one of Dad's favorites, "Danny Boy."

As I reviewed my father's letter, it occurred to me that leukemia was likely just shorthand, a succinct summary for the death certificate as a cause of death. I suspect there were additional unresolved, and unidentified factors. The cancer rate in our small farm town was high. Fertilizers and pesticides were routinely sprayed on nearby corn and bean fields. Not only that, but Dad so loved the insecticide dichlorobiphenyl trichloroethane (DDT) that he bought sacks of it before it was banned. Like many men of his generation, his relationship to DDT went back to his WWII experience, when the dusty white powder was the only thing that would rid your clothing and sleeping gear of vermin.

Then again, maybe Dad was just plain worn out. Once more, he was dealing with a job he didn't like, having become the acting head of Milford Canning

---

30   This man was humble and nonjudgmental. Of him, Mom said, "His sermons were written as if he was talking directly to me."

31   When asked about his religious beliefs, Dad said he didn't believe in God because he believed that any Father in heaven allowing his children on earth to suffer didn't merit worshipping.

32   As kids, we went to church regularly with my mother, but we were not a religious family. No praying at the dinner table and that sort of thing. But we were Anabaptists, meaning that we were "immersed in the watery grave" (baptized) when we were older, provided we confessed our sins publicly to the congregation. People often do a double take when I reveal this.

after Uncle Sam left. And my father was actively involved with launching three adult children: not an easy task, even for a man in good health. Then there were the "goddamn Illinois winters" as he described them. And the massive yard upkeep of a house he wanted to sell (or my mother wanted to sell). To add even more emotional burden, he was still dealing with two aging parents, then in their late eighties, and his father (my grandfather) was an especially cantankerous man.[33]

---

33   Two quick anecdotes about my grandfather involving guns. In his declining years, he asked my father to shoot him. My father quipped back, "Great, Dad. You're dead, and I go to jail." On one visit, Grandpa showed me the loaded pistol he kept underneath his pillow, which made me nervous. I told Uncle Sam, and he assured me, with a wink and a smile, that he'd loaded it with blanks a long time ago. My grandfather died while Dad was undergoing his first chemo, and thus there is no mention of him in the last few letters. His mother, Forrest Browne, survived him and, at the funeral, insisted that the minister, Forbes, mention some quote from Charles Lindbergh. (On his final Hawaii trip, my grandmother had insisted that Dad visit the Lindbergh grave in Hawaii, which he did.)

CHAPTER 4: PULLING IT TOGETHER

So far, I've summarized my father's letters, but, for the most part, I've not interpreted them through the lens of my own experience.[34] While I do believe the letters portray my father accurately, there is undoubtedly unconscious bias and skewed memory at play. Keep in mind that these letters were untouched for over thirty years, and when I looked at them, I had a fresh pair of eyes (no cataracts yet). When I read them, I was already five years older than my father had been when he died. This felt odd, being older than he was, but my seniority did give me a kind of permission to provide some additional commentary.

Historians consider personal letters as primary sources. Fair enough, but one could argue that objectivity suffers from the need to edit such personal

---

34   Of course, I did editorialize occasionally, as when I commented that Dad looked resigned in the snapshot from the Hawaiian hotel balcony.

letters. No readable history could possibly reprint every word of voluminous correspondence.[35] Nor would it help. Personal letters are, by their nature, personal, and they are intended to be read while still fresh. In this context, I freely admit to having edited Dad's letters. I chose what to put in and what to leave out. Perhaps this affects objectivity, if such a thing is even possible.

On the other hand, I did cross-check a few "facts" in the family history via my older cousin Jane Carroll and my longtime friend Bruce, whom you will learn more about in the final chapter.

One unheralded strength of the personal letter, especially in the case of my father's correspondence, is candidness. My father did not limit himself to a few noteworthy subjects.[36] I unquestionably accept his words as the truth—or at least his truth. There was no reason to mislead me in his letters. One beauty of these letters is their rawness, immediate even so many years later. And not just the words but the slapdash typing, the poor handwriting, the scratch outs. This was pure, free-form writing—unfiltered honesty. Free of pretense, free of self- editing.

Yet if there was one letter that struck me as disingenuous, it was his final one.

In the last letter he wrote me before his death, there is a bit of forced humor— something about his tormenting a salesclerk about purchasing fresh ammo and having left his traveler's checks in his getaway car. Perhaps this moment of levity was placed to lighten the bad news about returning to the hospital.

In the final paragraph, he advises my sister and me to stay at our jobs. For many years, this stuck with me. Dad had directed us to carry on and show up at work with an "obligation to career, job, and family." And his final line: "People resent extra work when you get sick and have no sympathy when it is a member of the family. This is the professional approach, and the way economic life is and should be." And he signed it "Doggie Daddy" (a Hanna-Barbera cartoon character), a sign-off he had never used previously. Another attempt to lighten the content perhaps?[37]

---

35   One exception to the rule are collections of letters from historical figures like presidents or major literary figures such as Flannery O'Connor. For them, complete collections are expected.

36   A disregard for any thought of what qualifies as a worthy topic is freeing for the writer.

37   But perhaps not. A couple of early readers of the manuscript, who are more familiar with the Hanna Barbera oeuvre than I, gave me some insights into the animated dachshund Doggie Daddy. Doggie Daddy's son, Augie Doggie, was often the focus of his father's attention, including slight reprimands for disappointing him. But in the end, Doggie

Dad's obligation to family made sense. But to think of him as someone who equated "valued career" with family—that just doesn't resonate. And none of his letters over the years hinted at such a philosophy. Quite the opposite, in fact, as he often commented that they called it "work" for a reason.[38]

Considering his grave condition, the message to just carry on was certainly noted by the then thirty-year-old me at the time. My youthful interpretation of his advice was simply "honor me by doing your job and not going to pieces." It was the advice that sustained me during years of intermittently unhappy employment. If there was ever any contradiction or disingenuousness in Dad's final advice, I know now it was no transgression. Unintended or not, Dad's advice comforted me for many years.

THE VIEW FROM HERE

Revisiting the letters has, as you would expect, led me to better understand my own life. This is more poignant, given that I'm significantly older now than my father was when he died. But reading, thinking about, and writing about them did not shift my worldview perceptibly. There were no Faulkner-size surprises in my family's past. Instead, spending time with the letters reaffirmed what I already knew but perhaps had not fully articulated. Here are some of my main takeaways.

THE WORLD OF WORK

In one of the letters, my father wrote, "I never did my best, but I never did my worst either." That resonated with much of my own employment experience.

If there is any one unsolved mystery to my father's life, it might be why he chose such a modest career path. After spending a few years in South Carolina, earning his undergraduate degree at The Citadel,[39] Dad then went to work

---

Daddy was very proud of his son, and he would turn to the camera and say affectionally in a Jimmy Durante–like voice (Durante is better known in this century as the narrator of the *Frosty the Snowman* Christmas TV special), "Dat's my boy who said dat." Hmmm. Maybe this does add some meaning to his final letter but maybe not.

38   Dad would have appreciated comedian Drew Carey's joke: "Oh, you hate your job? Why didn't you say so? There's a support group for that. It's called everybody, and they meet at the bar."

39   Almost equally perplexing is why my father went to a military college after being in the service since his war letters never indicated he thought the army was anything special. Two factors probably weighed in. The main one was that his brother was there,

at the Milford Canning Company. Not long after, he expended considerable effort commuting by train to the University of Chicago for his MBA, all with the responsibilities of supporting a young family.

As I mentioned earlier, my grandmother said that my father was not the same person when came back from the war, but she did not elaborate. Perhaps he was, by then, cynical, sad, or distrustful, but I can't be sure. After graduating from The Citadel, I do think he resolved never to stray far from home again. He preferred to simply tend his garden and eat at Bob Evans regularly.

He didn't have to be at his best because the Milford Canning Company never required it of him. He could do the accounting and financial oversight required with ease. His biggest challenge was finding the ability to tolerate his coworkers and the village trustees. Later he had to cope with his shifting relationship with his brother as they drifted apart, literally (my uncle Sam moved to the corporate headquarters in Ohio) and emotionally, since they were no longer as close as they once been.

As I see it now, my father was suspicious of anybody who was conventionally successful; he assumed it was achieved through nepotism, cutthroat tactics, or some other way to accumulate ill-gotten gains.

I've often wondered if his beliefs influenced my own relationship to the world of work. Until the last decade of my working life, when I held a conventional job in corporate America, my career was more a series of unrelated jobs, (product marketer, computer operator, feature writer-journalist, project manager, academic researcher[40]) than anything else.

A few short years before he died, my father did become what would now be called the chief operating officer (COO) of the Milford Canning Company. He was the head of the branch office (factory). While I can't say for certain, my guess is that he preferred to be in control at that point rather than having to train new people who would soon become his superiors. Similarly, this matched my own experience late in my work life. I didn't aspire to be a manager of a department until I was confident that it would be less stressful than having a

---

which indicated their closeness during those years. Secondly, at the military school where hazing underclassman was part of curriculum, WWII veterans were not subjected to hazing. (I could not verify this, but it makes sense.)

40   These are just the main jobs. I also had stints as an ad salesman for a country and western radio station, where I learned the art of fucking off while on the job; a clothing sales associate at Macy's who quit during the Christmas shopping season; a computer salesman who was fired; and a park groundskeeper who was yelled at by the supervisor for not "putting my heart into" cutting grass.

potentially incompetent supervisor managing my daily workload.

From reading his letters again, I found that my father's greatest fear seems to have been having an adult child return home unlaunched. To that end, there was continual encouragement in his letters. Other hardships would befall his adult children, but none ever did return home until after he died.

My father's attitudes about work and ambition have played a partial role in my own ambivalence about ambition and success.

A SENSE OF DUTY

What was clear after revisiting Dad's letters so many years later was his powerful sense of duty to his wife, his children, and also his aged parents.

At the time, of course, I was youthfully oblivious to any of this. My understanding of duty began when the first of my two daughters was born. The real test begins when you have the added responsibility of looking after an aging parent as well. When Mom fell on the ice while struggling with groceries, it became clear something had to change. Though my brother lived just ten minutes away, he offered no assistance to my mother as she recovered. Until then, I was unaware of her decline. Aging parents can fool you when only see them every so often.

When I moved my mother from Champaign, Illinois, to just across the street from me in metro Atlanta, I began to understand the fullness of family obligation. By then, Mom had been a widow for almost thirty years. And there were other painful losses along the way, including the death of my sister in 2005.

My mother suffered from anxiety, depression, and, later, an addiction to prescription drugs. And though I was slow to recognize it, dementia was setting in as well.[41] Her final decline—a broken hip and blindness in one eye—led to several overnight stays in the emergency room with her. My daughter Cynthia, in graduate school in Germany, was coincidentally dealing with baffling health problems of her own. This was a very stressful time for me as well, having finally worked my way into a full-time managerial job with many responsibilities. I clearly remember waiting for the train ride home after work feeling exhausted, thinking, *I cannot take another step.* But in times like these, I would think of my father and his "march or die" ethic. You might think such motivation overly

---

41   At first, I thought she was just being difficult. I'm told this is typical in such circumstances.

dramatic, but it has, at times, helped me put that next foot forward. I knew my father would be proud of me for stepping up to take care of Mom. To my father, a career meant nothing if you neglected your loved ones.

I am obligated to say here that I loved my mother. She was a dedicated, supportive mother to her children (near the point of being a Serial Mom[42]), but I wouldn't say we were close. Nor were we distant. We had more of a middle-of-the-road relationship. As many have discovered, when you care for an aging parent, it reveals what that relationship really is.

It took time and careful effort to manage Mom's affairs. I'm not proud to admit that I did lose patience with her a few times, once yelling at her in an empty mall. My mother was never an easy person; she was like the family Welsh terrier who would lock its jaws and just repeatedly shake its prey, never letting go until it was dead (or feigned death). Mom simply didn't let go of things very well.

It was then that I took a hard look at myself. I realized I didn't want to be the type of person who raised his voice at his mother. I needed a coping mantra.

For me, this is when your sense of duty—an obligation to the role of being a son or a father—takes over. You do it because that is what you expect of yourself. *Love is not required.*[43] I just did it without spending a lot of time thinking about it, and now I am certain my father influenced this self-expectation. In his letters, Dad was always casual about how he would leave early on a weekend or during his lunch hour to handle one crisis after another for his parents. And such unscheduled visits were in addition to his regular weekly trips.[44] He wrote:

> Mother asked me to come down Saturday morning as her leg hurt her and Dad wasn't able to get to the barn to take care of the Cluck-Clucks as well as move Miss Kitty [the name they gave to their cat in honor of the saloon madam character in their favorite

42   John Waters's film *Serial Mom* is a 1994 black comedy starring Kathleen Turner as a protective mother who murders the rivals of her teenage children.

43   My longtime friend Bill, one of the early reviewers of this manuscript, commented extensively about the relationship between duty and love. He wrote, "Sometimes, it is love that propels duty, and with duty come self-sacrifice."

44   I could never remember a time, that Dad didn't drive the eleven miles every Tuesday night after supper to visit his parents. Later, when I was in high school, I often went with him. I was welcome to go, and I think that I just liked being with him. He probably liked the company during the drive. I would visit my grandparents, bring my homework or a book, and just hang out and listen. Later this paid off big time because they gave me their old car—a 1961 Buick Electra—when I was a high school junior.

television show, *Gunsmoke*] and the kittens to the barn.

In another instance:

> Went down at noon with Sam as Mother called in tears and said, "Dad was dying and wanted to see at least one of us." She had given him a pain pill and he fell asleep when we got there and looked like some baby doing time in a maternity ward.

It's been my observation that children caring for aging parents often feel guilty; there's an expectation they should have warm fuzzies while they clean up the orange juice that spilled on the kitchen floor the previous day. As I see it, as long as that frustration doesn't boil over into anger and you're not raising your voice, you are doing just fine.

A SENSE OF HUMOR

It's not easy to categorize Dad's sense of humor. But he did have one, and it occasionally reached beyond just enclosing cartoons and newspaper clips in his letters. Here's his "review" of an evening at the American Legion:

> Had a nice evening Friday night at the Legion in Hoopeston, Bruce M. was to play guitar for several hours as the entertainment following the weekly fish fry. Joanne and Jack, Bill & Inna Mae,[45] [Bruce's brother] Rick M. and his new wife, grandmother and aunt of Bruce and Rick's made up the cheering section. I think "show biz" has to be the toughest of all routes, but it is even tougher to sing all your own songs all evening in a barroom filled with fish and beer filled patrons. We were in the cheering section, but he should realize that only Mothers and Grandmothers can think, [that Bruce's song] "Getting Together at the Railroad Bar in Villa Grove" is commercial. The lyrics may have changed for each presentation, but for two and a half hours we heard the same melody. No Willie Nelson, he, and with the same tune who is to know if he can play?

And another example:

> I was enjoying a nice homemade corn bread muffin and inhaled a crumb that choked me. Jean took positive action and thumped me on the back causing the crumb to come loose in time. Charlie [the family dog] took positive action and ate my supper at the

---

45   Joanne, Jack, Bill, and Inna Mae were my aunts and uncles on my mother's side. Rick and Bruce were Inna Mae's sons.

height of the action. Could have forgiven him for that, but the little piggly begged for some of my second supper.

For light comic effect throughout his letters, perhaps unknowingly, he'd give people, places, and things alternative satirical names. I was often called something other than Murray. Once he suggested he'd forgotten my real name! His most-used salutation was "Zonker," after the free-spirited, hippie character in Gary Trudeau's comic strip *Doonesbury*. I had no quarrel with this and, in fact, once presented Dad with a copy of *Tales from the Margaret Mead Taproom* by Nicholas Von Hoffman, illustrated with cartoons by Trudeau. The book chronicles the adventures of Zonker after he joined Uncle Duke (Trudeau's parody of Hunter S. Thompson) when Duke was appointed ambassador to American Samoa.

There was more humor in Dad's letters, but much of it was scattershot,[46] often missing its mark. For Dad, sharing the daily inanities of his life with me was a way of handling all the crap he put up with over the years. In a broader sense, with the help of humor, his letter writing may have been simply a coping mechanism.

While he liked to laugh in social situations (and sometimes at the office), he was not the comedian at home. Mom said he was not so much of a hardy-har-har guy around the house. It wasn't that he was prone to broodiness or distance, but his letters were much more revealing. The father I remember sitting in his favorite chair and the narrator of the letters seemed, at times, to be different people. What he revealed in his letters were thoughts and musings he would never say directly in conversing with his family at home. And I treasure this now—his candid asides, written with spontaneity, which bring him to life as I reread the letters.

My father's letters have cadence and energy. He had what all good writers must have—his own voice.

MY OWN LETTERS

As my father did with me, I wrote to my daughter Cynthia while she was an undergraduate at Rice University in Houston. At the outset, I referred to these letters as My Banal Life. The rules were simple: no judgement should be put forth with respect to spelling or grammar. And no topic could be too banal. This permitted a wide range of subject matter. Had I been focused on weighty

---

46   And some of the humor was poor taste, especially by today's standards.

matters, such as current events or the raw, fresh feelings from my divorce, which was finalized during Cynthia's first year in college, then I would not have written much at all. Instead, I freely regaled Cynthia with the small details of daily life at what I called the Broken Lives Apartments, a name I chose because the typical tenants were either recently divorced middle-aged adults or senior citizens. Sometimes I would send the letters by post. Sometimes I emailed them. (In keeping with tradition, Cynthia would print them before reading.) She has kept many of the letters, and there were almost a hundred of them.

CHAPTER 5: LESSONS LEARNED

In the winter of 1983–1984, a few months before my father was first diagnosed with leukemia, I quit my product-marketing job at a computer company to pursue a master of arts in gerontology, the study of aging. Normally, an eighteen-month educational sidetrack like this might seem unremarkable, but it later proved to be the beginning of a major shift in my thinking that changed my life from that point forward.

When I telephoned my father back in rural Illinois to say that I was going to quit my job, he replied, "You want to get a degree in gerontology? Why don't you try spending more time with your grandparents?" This clearly demonstrated his bludgeoning bluntness, which could be funny when it wasn't aimed at you.[47]

STUDYING AGING AS A YOUTH, EXPLAINED

My future ex-wife and I were working full-time jobs in Wichita, Kansas, in 1982 when our first daughter, Cynthia, was born. Like most men at that time, I assumed (incorrectly) that my wife would stay home with our daughter. However, it soon became obvious that she was temperamentally ill suited for domestic life. Instead, she anxiously wanted to return to full-time work as a math instructor at Wichita State University. When that happened, our infant daughter went into full-time day care. I soon began to feel guilty that Cynthia was in day care too much, and we decided, after entering couples therapy, that I would quit my job and go to graduate school. This was an unconventional career path for a man in the early 1980s.

The main influencer in this decision was our therapist, Bruce.[48] Before my

---

47   Though it did not lessen the sting of his words, I understood my father's point of view. I was going from what would be considered a well-paid position with a future (computers) to a position that was more like social work and did not promise financial security.

48   After my father, Bruce was the most influential man in my life. Back in the mid-1980s, he recognized my nontraditional side and encouraged me to pursue my bookish curiosities (part of the shift in my thinking). Forty years later, Bruce and I still exchange books

future ex-wife dropped out of therapy, she commented that "Murray likes old people." I did not deny this. And it wasn't just that I spent many hours with my grandparents as a youth.

Not only did I spend time growing up near my grandparents but also, in 1977, just after college, my cousin Rick and I rented a "penthouse" apartment in the declining industrial town of Danville, Illinois. This five-story, red-brick building, built in the boom times of the 1920s, was known as the Holland and featured Flemish-revival architecture with its distinctive stepped gables. Adjacent to the Holland was a Holiday Inn. This was during the hotel's mid-century boom as the Nation's Innkeeper. It had distinctive signage—a four-story monstrous thing with green lettering topped with a pink, white, and blue neon star that flashed continually throughout the day and night. One benefit of this magnificent sign was that, after dark, it bathed our living room in a pastel rainbow of light. Exotic!

Aside from us, the apartment building was inhabited entirely by senior citizens. At the main entrance, there were two rows of chairs on each side of the hallway. From morning to evening, the older residents rotated in and out of these chairs. We called them "the Gauntlet" as their inquiring gazes sized up our every entry and departure from the Holland. But once the Gauntlet figured out that our idea of raucous night activity was playing frisbee on the nearly dead outdoor mall downtown, we were accepted. I should add that after my time at the Holland, I wrote an unpublished, single-spaced, 250-page novel, *Souls in Flux*, about the experience.[49]

The Holland was not only cheap, but it also was roomy and convenient. I recall it fondly. Before we married, my ex-wife visited me there often, so she knew how comfortable I was around seniors.

Bruce picked up on my wife's remark and suggested that I consider the gerontology program at Wichita State University. It would be an interesting change for me and potentially less demanding than a full-time job. The school, with its many commuter students, also had affordable on-site day care. Many of the classes met only once or twice each week.

One takeaway from my time in the gerontology classroom was the social theory that what you did to earn your living greatly affected your adjustment to retirement. If you were a high-status professional (doctor, lawyer, teacher,

---

and ideas.

49   There is only one copy of this book, printed on a dot-matrix printer, and it is three-hole punched into a used binder. It resides in the same closet as my father's letters.

engineer, or wealthy entrepreneur), it may, in fact, diminish your post-work well-being. You might assume people are still going to honor your former status, but this is rarely the case. Most people don't care what you did before you retired and are disinclined to hear you talk about it. And if your work provided much of your life focus, you might have an emotional void that is unfilled in retirement.

On the other hand, retirees who didn't like their jobs often have far less trouble adjusting. This would have been my father's case had he lived long enough to retire.

During my time at Wichita State University, I read Sharon R. Kaufmann's *The Ageless Self: Sources of Meaning in Later Life*. This differentiates those who leverage their occupation into meaningfulness in their later lives from those who do not. She writes:

> For about half of the study group, work was something that had to be done and it never provided much satisfaction. Other aspects of life such as family relations or friendships hold much more meaning. For others, especially those with professions, the work role has been a primary source of identity, and occupational achievements have been the main source of gratification and positive self-esteem. . . Those who were heavily invested in their occupations define the successes and failures in their lives in terms of their jobs and describe themselves in terms of occupational roles and work habits.

STUDYING AGING: A REFRESHER COURSE

As I mentioned in Chapter 1, after I returned from a three-week trip to Europe, I went to the career counseling service center, knowing that I would have to deal with my discomfort of being in new environments and situations. I was surrounded by people who were more dedicated to finding a job than I, since finances dictated that I could retire.

I expected that these career coaches would think of us as nothing more than commodities—our personal stories of obsolescence to be easily brushed aside with nods and let's-move-on attitudes, but my counselor, Russell, was different. At least he was near my age and acknowledged that not all of us necessarily needed to go back to a full- time job. (He understood!) He introduced me to the phrase "active retirement." In our one on one, he said that he was at the stage in his own career that he only did the part of the job that he liked. He preferred working with individuals to soliciting businesses to handle their outplacing of employees. I appreciated his own self- awareness.

This reminded me of the days when I was a feature writer for a monthly senior citizen newspaper putting together a story about retired ministers. The premise of the article was "If you decided to become a minister because of a calling from God, how could you possibly retire?" This was a trick question, but what I found out from the retired ministers was that, in retirement, they pursued only the aspects of ministering that they liked (preaching, theological scholarship, ministering to the sick, or counseling) and avoided the awful tasks such as being a church administrator.[50]

That story had always stuck with me, and I recognized that quality in Russell. He was doing part of the job that he enjoyed, and I wanted to follow his lead.

What was funny was that, in my 12-year corporate tenure, I had written two books, including a book of essays, *The Book Shopper: A Life in Review*. I blogged incessantly as well, but only a few of my work colleagues knew anything about this.[51] However, I must have given off a vibe that I was not all in. When one of the women in our department left our group, she said in parting, "You drank the corporate Kool-Aid, but you spat it out when no one was looking." I am my father's son.

However, shifting from corporate middle manager to potential retiree (I say potential because I was not absolutely sure even then that I wouldn't go back to work) was not some sort of on-off switch. At first, I resisted giving up the career and tried to incorporate my former life of performance reviews and the collecting of annual bonuses with my writer-blogger-bookseller self[52], who did not make enough in the latter endeavors to cover paper supplies.

Russell emphasized the idea that whether it's your resume or your LinkedIn

---

50   When I reread the February 1994 article, I was more impressed with the three ministers I had interviewed. They were way ahead of me, and they had the "calling" issue resolved. They acknowledged that some ministers had lost their way, but "the calling" was not necessarily one of those Moses-and-the-burning-bush kind of moments. Said one retired minister, "You must live for a cause that is bigger than yourself. That's true for all vocations."

51   The Book Shopper blog (thebookshopper.org) began in 2008. In 2023, I posted my 500th entry.

52   Within a month of being packaged out, I came up with an idea to start my own book pop-up business called Destination: Books. Three years later, it continues grow. Ironically, I have taken book shopping to a new level by scouting for and purchasing books for the pop-up.

profile, you needed a cohesive narrative. "Tell your story," he said, but what he really meant is that you can't have it both ways. I appreciated his advice because when I used to interview and hire people, I would always look for a narrative on their resume. That would give me a sense of whether our department was a good match for the next chapter in the interviewee's career.

By my final session, I began to let go of my former professional life. It was a relief. Russell and I ended my outplacement course on a positive note, joking about what I was supposed to do with the ream of linen resume paper I had in a storage cabinet. "Oh yes, we get that once in a while," said Russell.

Also, during this time, I reread my tattered paperback copy of the Kaufmann book and another premise of hers stood out. She maintained that retired people find more meaning in their lives when they understand there have been patterns to their behavior and activities. These patterns were formed in their jobs/careers or the extracurriculars outside their jobs and careers, and all reflect their interests and personalities.

PATTERNS FROM THE CLOSET

It took some additional time ruminating about personal patterns before I realized that writing, blogging, bookselling, and even publishing had been a part of my life since time immemorial—dating back to my fifth grade work on English-language literature, *Great Authors*.

There was the satire of my high school newspaper (one copy), a vulgar dorm newspaper in college (we used the residence office copier after hours), an awful collection of writing called *After-Dinner Mints*. ("If literature was a full-course meal, who would provide the after-dinner mints?") This didn't end with college, marriage, or children. In my baseball-nerdy stage, I wrote and self-published two pamphlets on baseball statistics, which led to other opportunities, including a regular column entitled "Life in the Sticks" (stat-tis-sticks) in a gorgeously printed, short-lived, and doomed baseball literary magazine, *Elysian Fields Quarterly*.

The desire to write and publish runs deep and for my 60th birthday instead of making a bucket list trip I chose to write a novel-as-screenplay-as-novel about my experiences riding the subways of the Metropolitan Atlanta Rapid Transit Authority. The same do-it yourself-your- way creative mentality of my younger days spawned *Down & Outbound: A Mass Transit Satire*. I hardly

bothered looking for a publisher, because it was unlikely that anyone was going to publish the book in the format I desired. (In my promotional video which is on YouTube says it was designed for the commuter to read with one hand while holding on to the "oh-shit" bars with the other.) Despite all this effort, the book sold like cold cakes.[53]

For the most part *A Father's Letters* is just my continuation of "writers are gonna write" and "gonna get published somehow" pattern that I have established since the elementary school days of *Great Authors*. But this book serves other purposes as well.

The more personal revelation was not that I had been a writer since my salad days, but that my father—a writer himself (just not published)—understood we were both compelled to write. I like to think he recognized that in me and thus felt comfortable sending all those letters. (He must have gotten the hint of my bookish ways when, as an undergraduate, I dropped my business minor in favor of adding English as part of a double major.) He was too practical to ever encourage a writing career, but he must have appreciated that we shared the same drive to chronicle "our life and times." It didn't matter so much that his son couldn't fix a washing machine.

And finally, to those readers on the cusp of retirement and new retirees who have started wondering, *Well, what next?* Your thoughts may even be drifting away right now to your archive of photos, letters, and videos. Why not dig in? You may uncover some personal wisdom today to assist you in the years

---

53   Copies of *Down & Outbound* and my other works such *Souls in Flux*, and *Great Authors* and quarterlies containing my "Life in the Sticks" essays continue, in some form or another, to inhabit the same closet/archives that housed my father's letters. In my post-publication sales analytics of *Down & Outbound*, I determined that the book was a little "too arty" for the common reader and "not arty enough" for the book-art elitists. I had found the perfect sour spot.

ahead. It's never too late for a little self-discovery. It belongs right up there with exercising for good health and saving for your financial security.

Please accept this memoir as a series of notes, something you might borrow from a trusted classmate in college when you didn't bother to go to lecture. Or it can be, as Thomas Pynchon writes in the introduction to his book of essays *Slow Learner*, just "another case of what Frank Zappa calls a bunch of old guys sitting around playing rock 'n' roll. But as we all know, rock 'n' roll will never die, and education too...keeps on going on forever."

APPENDIX A

**Glenn R. Browne
(1893-1984)
m. Forrest Murray
(1898-1988)**

**Samuel P. Browne
(1924-2014)
m. "Bette" Carroll
(1926-2016)**

**Glenn R. Browne Jr.
(1925-1985)
m. Clara Jean Burtis
(1927-2013)**

Jane Carroll Browne
(1948 -)
Hunter Schenk (1982 -)

Neil Browne
(1952-2017)

Murray Browne
(1955 -)
Cynthia Jean Browne (1982 -)
Bonnie Elaine Poore (1987 -)

Kay Browne
(1958-2005)
Tristan Glenn Honn (1987 -)
Sadie Elizabeth Shell (1990 -)

Browne Branch of
Family Tree

APPENDIX B

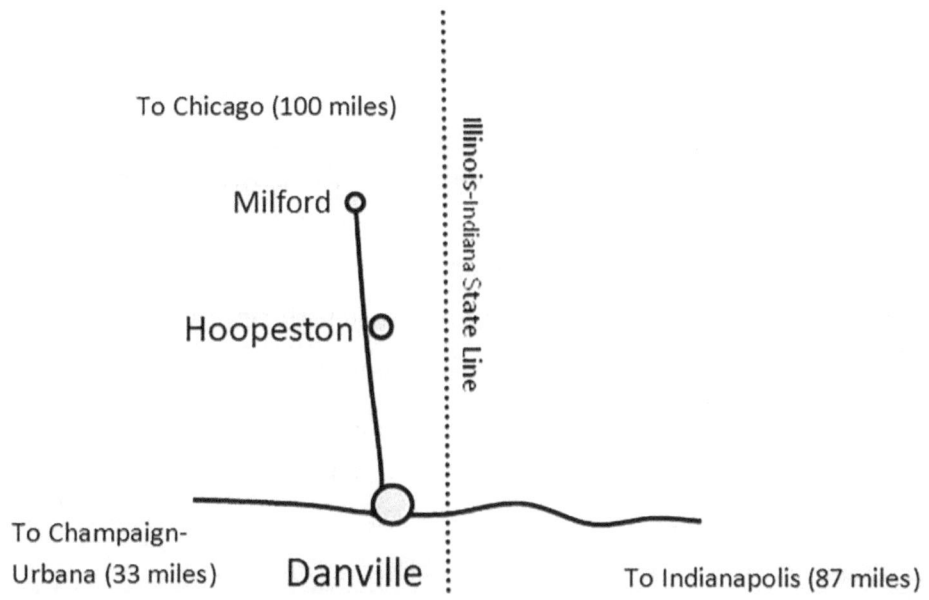

Where is Milford, Illinois?

PHOTO AND ART CREDITS

Unless specifically attributed, photos and art were taken, drawn, or scanned by the author. The exceptions:

Front cover: "You Can't Lay Down Your Memory Chest of Drawers" with permission Tejo Remy. © Tejo Remy. Photo by Mike Jensen, courtesy of High Museum of Art, Atlanta.

Glenn Browne Infantryman - (photographer unknown, 1945).

Stamaty Cartoon – Mark Alan Stamaty, reprinted with permission.

Cotham Cartoon – Cartoonstock.com with permission.

Glenn with Kay, Murray and Cynthia (photographer Clara Jean Browne, 1984).

Glenn with Jean/Glenn on Balcony in Hawaii (photographer unknown, 1985).

Back cover: Author photo (Denise Casey, 2022).

Manuscript formatting and layout: Audrey Hoisington

Cover design: Dina Klarisse Dugar

ACKNOWLEDGEMENTS

Again, I relied on the critical reading of early drafts of those who have been part of the process. They include Wally Leisering, Bill Gwin, Francis Walker, and Bruce Woods. Dave Dintenfass provided invaluable line editing, proofreading and editorial suggestions to make the manuscript presentable. Warren Farha of Eighth Day Books provided a shot of encouragement along the way, which reinforced that what I had written was something meaningful.

My long-time partner Denise Casey has been a patient supporter, editor, and sounding board for my writing and my life for twenty-three years. I realize that this can sometimes be a labor of love, but with an emphasis on love. In this book, there is a mention of her father, Mickey Koslow, and I was glad to have a small way to honor Denise's family, which has been important to me in my later years, especially since my mother, father, sister, and brother have all passed away.

It's strange that I am the only one left to tell the story of our immediate family. (But my older cousin, Jane Carroll Browne, has provided some key details—thanks, JC). Part of me always must write about what I am experiencing at the time. This book was different because I often thought about my daughters, Cynthia and Bonnie, as I wrote. With one brief exception, they never met their grandfather, and now, well, he's an open book—at least as far as I knew him. Maybe my grandsons Myrick and Larson will be interested in some family history along the way, too.

I also thought of my nephew Tristan Honn and niece Sadie Shell, who never met their grandfather either. Knowing something about family history is important, but I am not sure obsessing is such a healthy idea.

Finally, understanding something about one's family history is useful, but I am someone who believes at some point you must try to keep moving forward in your own life.

Decatur, Georgia

August 2023